HAL•LEONARD
BASS
PLAY-ALONG

AUDIO ACCESS INCLUDED

VOL. 1

ROCK

T0055324

PLAYBACK+
Speed • Pitch • Balance • Loop

To access audio visit:
www.halleonard.com/mylibrary

Enter Code
5533-6005-9761-2322

ISBN 978-0-634-08997-8

HAL•LEONARD®
7777 W. BLUEMOUND RD. P.O. BOX 13819 MILWAUKEE, WI 53213

Visit Hal Leonard Online at
www.halleonard.com

contents

Bass Notation Legend

Bass music can be notated two different ways: on a *musical staff*, and in *tablature*

THE MUSICAL STAFF shows pitches and rhythms and is divided by bar lines into measures. Pitches are named after the first seven letters of the alphabet.

TABLATURE graphically represents the bass fingerboard. Each horizontal line represents a string, and each number represents a fret.

3rd string, open   2nd string, 2nd fret   1st & 2nd strings open, played together

HAMMER-ON: Strike the first (lower) note with one finger, then sound the higher note (on the same string) with another finger by fretting it without picking.

PULL-OFF: Place both fingers on the notes to be sounded. Strike the first finger and without picking, pull the finger off to sound the second (lower) note.

LEGATO SLIDE: Strike the first note and then slide the same fret-hand finger up or down to the second note. The second note is not struck.

SHIFT SLIDE: Same as legato slide, except the second note is struck.

TRILL: Very rapidly alternate between the notes indicated by continuously hammering on and pulling off.

TREMOLO PICKING: The note is picked as rapidly and continuously as possible.

VIBRATO: The string is vibrated by rapidly bending and releasing the note with the fretting hand.

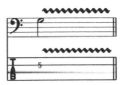

SHAKE: Using one finger, rapidly alternate between two notes on one string by sliding either a half-step above or below.

NATURAL HARMONIC: Strike the note while the fret hand lightly touches the string directly over the fret indicated.

MUFFLED STRINGS: A percussive sound is produced by laying the fret hand across the string(s) without depressing them and striking them with the pick hand.

BEND: Strike the note and bend up the interval shown.

BEND AND RELEASE: Strike the note and bend up as indicated, then release back to the original note. Only the first note is struck.

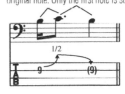

RIGHT-HAND TAP: Hammer ("tap") the fret indicated with the "pick-hand" index or middle finger and pull off to the note fretted by the fret hand.

LEFT-HAND TAP: Hammer ("tap") the fret indicated with the "fret-hand" index or middle finger.

SLAP: Strike ("slap") string with right-hand thumb.

POP: Snap ("pop") string with right-hand index or middle finger.

Additional Musical Definitions

    (accent)   • Accentuate note (play it louder)

Fill   • Label used to identify a brief pattern which is to be inserted into the arrangement.

    (accent)   • Accentuate note with great intensity

    • Repeat measures between signs.

    (staccato)   • Play the note short

D.S. al Coda   • Go back to the sign (%), then play until the measure marked *"To Coda"*, then skip to the section labelled *"Coda."*

   • When a repeated section has different endings, play the first ending only the first time and the second ending only the second time.

5

Another One Bites the Dust

Words and Music by John Deacon

oth - er one bites the dust. __ And an - oth - er one gone, and an - oth - er one gone. An -

oth - er one bites the dust, __ yeah. Hey, I'm gon - na get you too. An -

oth - er one bites the dust. __

Ah, ___ take it!   Bite the dust! ___   Bite the dust, ___

___ ah!   Hey!   An -

Bridge

N.C.

oth - er one bites the dust. ___   An - oth - er one bites the dust. ___ Ow! ___   An -

oth - er one bites the dust. ___ Hey, hey! ___   An - oth - er one bites the dust. ___ Hey. ___

5   3

(Em)   (Am)

0   0   0   0   0   0   3   0   5

Hey, I'm gon-na get you too. An-oth-er one bites the dust. ___

Shoot - out! ___

Ay. ___

Al - right. ___

Badge

Words and Music by Eric Clapton and George Harrison

Intro
Moderately slow Rock ♩ = 106

1. Think-in' 'bout the times you drove in my car.

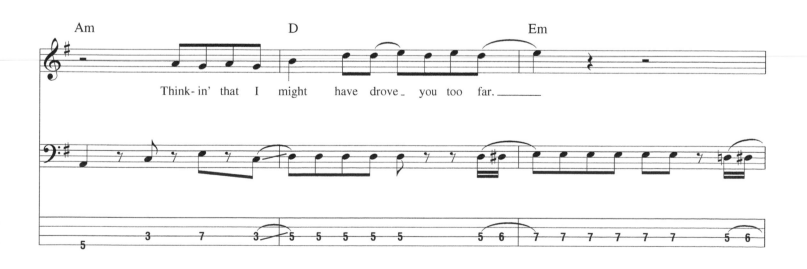

Think-in' that I might have drove you too far.

they bring the cur - tain down. ___   Yes, be - fore ___ they bring the cur - tain down. ___

Guitar Solo

Verse

3. Talk - in' 'bout a girl that looks ___ quite like you.

She did - n't have the time to wait ___ in the queue. ___

She cried a - way her

life since she fell off the cra - dle.

Brown Eyed Girl

Words and Music by Van Morrison

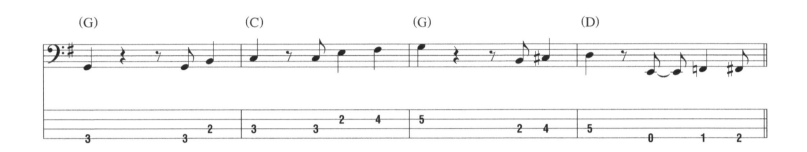

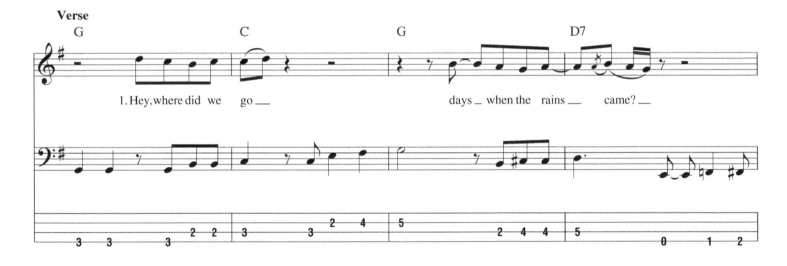

1. Hey, where did we go ___ days ___ when the rains ___ came? ___

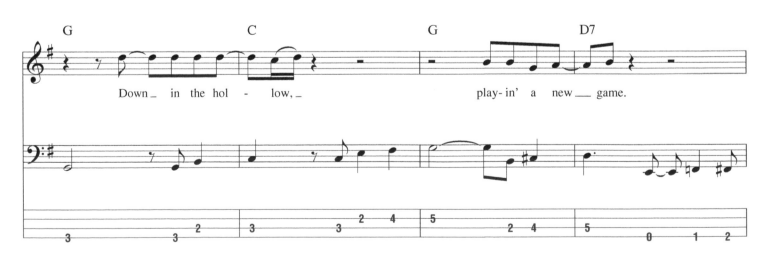

Down ___ in the hol - low, ___ play-in' a new ___ game.

Verse

2. Now, what-ev-er hap - pened to Tues - day and so ___ slow?

Go-ing down the old ___ mine with a tran - sis - tor ra - di - o.

Stand-ing in the sun-light laugh - ing, hid - ing be-hind ___ a

rain-bow's wall. ___ Slip-ping and a slid - ing all a-long the

Sha, la, ___ la, la, ___ la, la, la, la, ___ la, la, la, te, da. ___ La, te, da. ___

Bass Interlude

N.C. (G)　　　(C)　　　(G)　　　(D7)

Verse

3. So hard to find ___ my way now ___ that I'm all ___

___ on my ___ own. ___ I saw you just ___ the oth-er day; ___

24

Come Together

Words and Music by John Lennon and Paul McCartney

Intro
Moderately slow Rock ♩ = 84

Interlude

Whispered:

Verse

you know_ me."_ One thing I can tell you is you got to be free._ Come to-geth-

Chorus

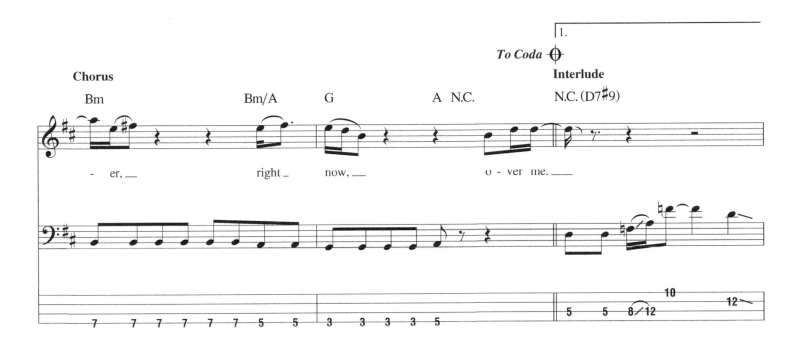

- er,_ right_ now,_ o-ver me._

Interlude

Whispered:
Shoot me. Shoot me. Shoot me.

Coda

Interlude

Whispered: Shoot me.

Shoot me.

Outro

w/ Voc. ad lib., till fade

N.C. (D7#9)

Shoot me.

Oh!

Repeat and fade

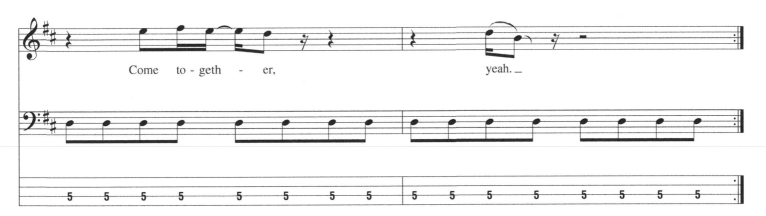

Come to - geth - er,

yeah.

Additional Lyrics

3. He bag production, he got walrus gumboot.
   He got ono sideboard, he one spinal cracker.
   He got feet down below his knee.
   Hold you in his armchair, you can feel his disease.

4. He rollercoaster, he got early warning.
   He got muddy water, he one Mojo filter,
   He say, "One and one and one is three."
   Got to be good lookin' 'cause he's so hard to see.

The Joker

Words and Music by Steve Miller, Eddie Curtis and Ahmet Ertegun

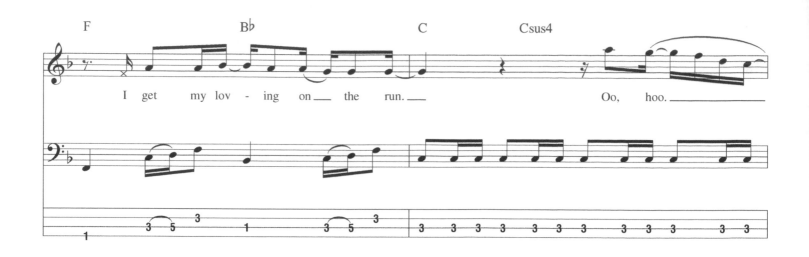

I get my lov - ing on the run. Oo, hoo.

Guitar Solo

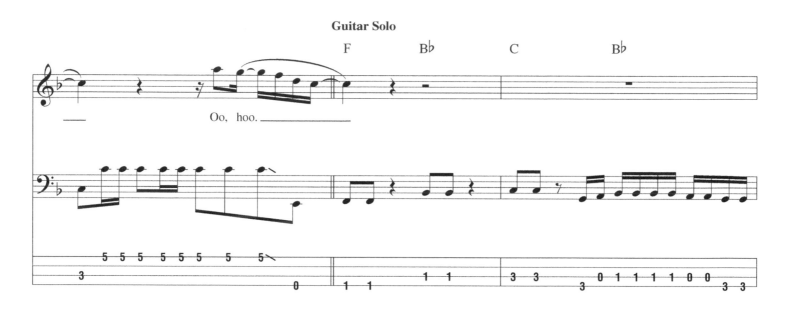

Oo, hoo.

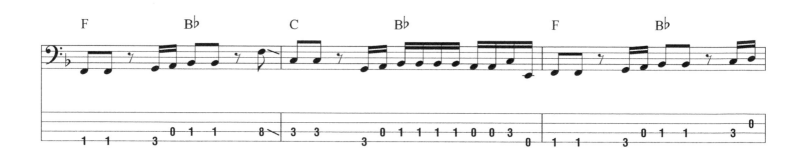

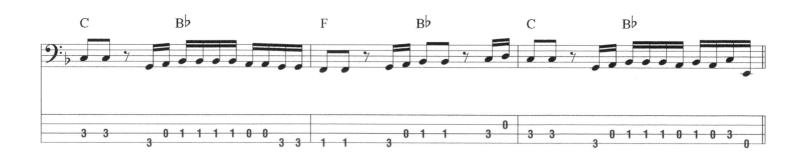

Verse

2. You're the cut - est thing _ that I ev - er did see. _____ I

real - ly love _ your peach - es, want to shake your tree. _____

Love - y dove - y, love - y dove- y, love - y dove-y all the time. _____

D.S. al Coda

Oo, wee, ba - by, I'll sure show you a good time. _____ 'Cause I'm a

Coda

I sure   don't want_ to   hurt_   no   one. _____

Guitar Solo

Oo,   hoo. _____   Oo,   hoo. _____

Outro-Verse
w/ Voc. ad lib. on repeat

Low Rider

Words and Music by Sylvester Allen, Harold R. Brown, Morris Dickerson,
Jerry Goldsmith, Leroy Jordan, Lee Oskar, Charles W. Miller and Howard Scott

1. All my friends know the low
2., 3., 4. *See additional lyrics*

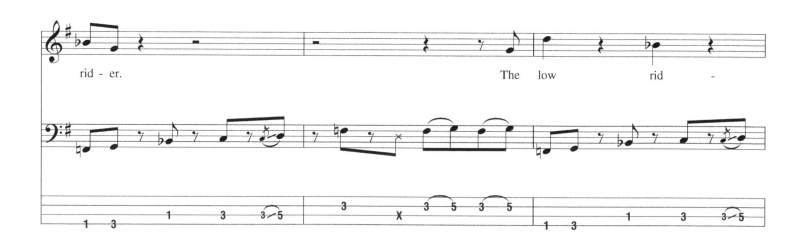

rid - er. The low rid -

er   is   a lit - tle high - er.

Chorus

N.C. (G7)

Play 4 times

Outro

N.C. (G7)

Take a lit - tle trip,   take a lit - tle trip,   take a lit - tle trip   and   see. _____

Take a lit-tle trip, take a lit-tle trip, take a lit-tle trip with me.

Repeat and fade

Additional Lyrics

2. Low rider drives a little slower.
Low rider, he's a real goer.

3. Low rider knows ev'ry street, yeah.
Low rider is the one to meet, yeah.

4. Low rider don't use no gas now.
Low rider don't drive too fast.

Money

Words and Music by Roger Waters

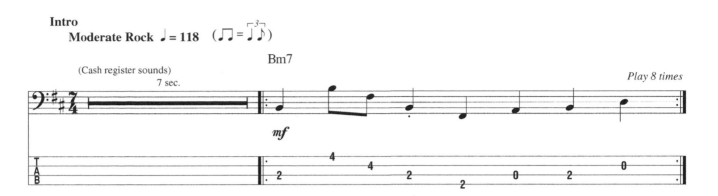

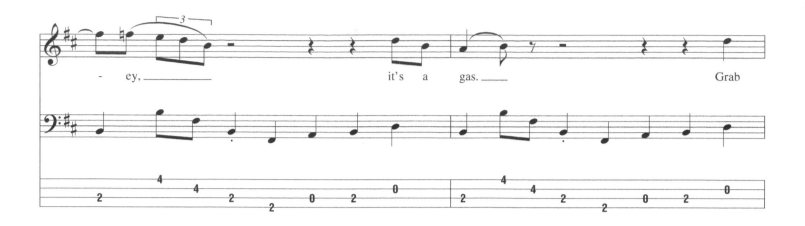

-ey, _____ it's a gas. _____ Grab

that cash with both hands and make a stash.

To Coda ⊕

F#m

Em7

New car, cav - i - ar, four star day - dream. Think I'll buy me a foot - ball ___

Bm7

_____ team.

44

Saxophone Solo

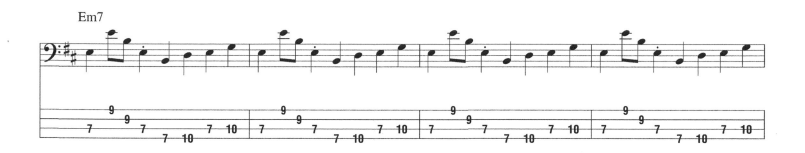

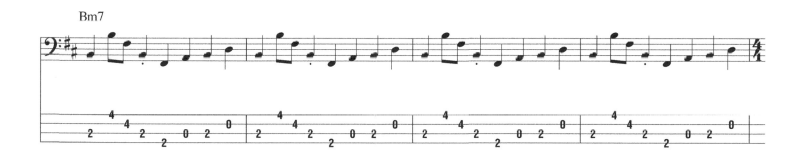

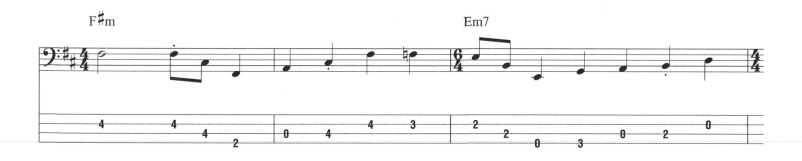

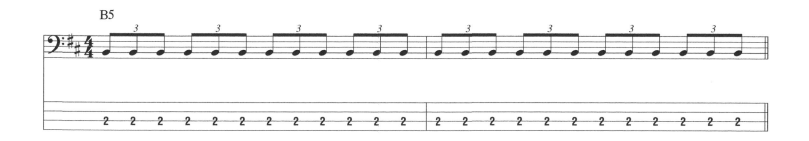

Guitar Solo

*Slur to 1st B note on repeats.

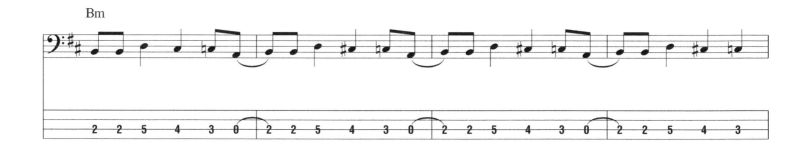

D.S. al Coda

⊕ Coda

Outro

Repeat and fade

w/ Voc. ad lib., till fade

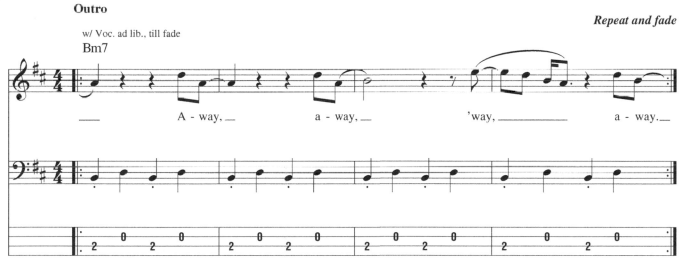

A - way, ___   a - way, ___   'way, _____   a - way. ___

Additional Lyrics

2. Money, well, get back.
   I'm all right, Jack, keep your hands off of my stack.
   Money, it's a hit.
   Ah, don't give me that do goody good bullshit.
   I'm in the high fidelity first class traveling
   Set, and I think I need a Lear jet.

3. Money, it's a crime.
   Share it fairly, but don't take a slice of my pie.
   Money, so they say,
   Is the root of all evil today.
   But if you ask for a rise it's no surprise
   That they're giving none away.

Sweet Emotion

Words and Music by Steven Tyler and Tom Hamilton

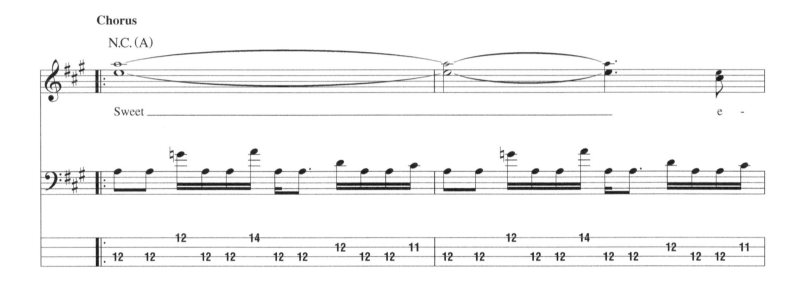

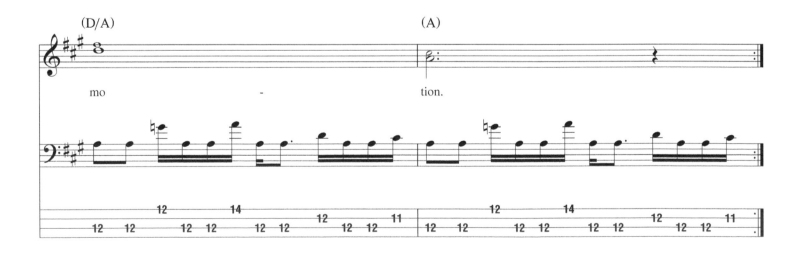

% **Verse**

1. Talk a-bout things and no - bod - y cares,   you're
3. *See additional lyrics*

wear-in' out things that no - bod - y wears.   You're

call-in' my name, but I got-ta make   clear,   I

can't say, ba - by, where I'll be in a year.

Interlude

2. Some

Verse

2nd time, substitute Fill 1, 4 times

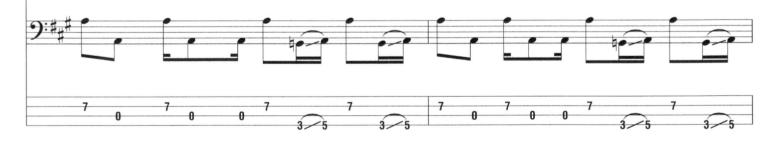

sweet - talk - in' ma - ma with a face like a gent   said my

4. *See additional lyrics*

Fill 1

To Coda ⊕

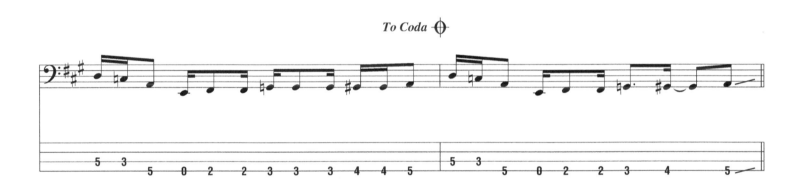

Chorus

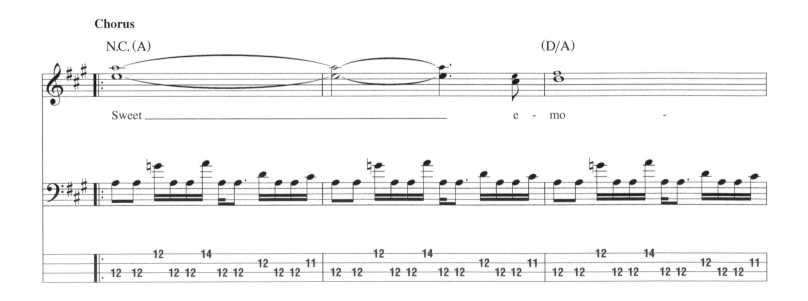

Sweet _____ e - mo -

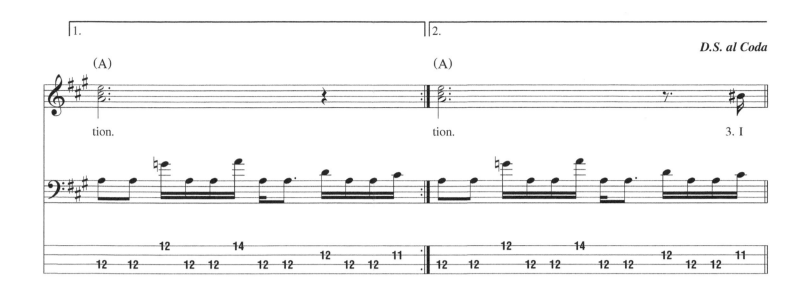

Coda

Outro

Play 12 times and fade

N.C. (E7)

Additional Lyrics

3. I pulled into town in a police car;
   You daddy said I took you just a little too far.
   You're tellin' her things but your girlfriend lied;
   You can't catch me 'cause the rabbit done died.

4. Stand in front just a shakin' your ass;
   I'll take you backstage, you can drink from my glass.
   I'm talkin' 'bout somethin' you can sure understand,
   'Cause a month on the road and I'll be eatin' from your hand.

Hal•Leonard® BASS PLAY-ALONG

The Bass Play-Along™ Series will help you play your favorite songs quickly and easily! Just follow the tab, listen to the audio to hear how the bass should sound, and then play-along using the separate backing tracks. The melody and lyrics are also included in the book in case you want to sing, or to simply help you follow along. The audio files are enhanced so you can adjust the recording to any tempo without changing pitch!

Visit Hal Leonard Online at **www.halleonard.com**

Prices, contents, and availability subject to change without notice.

HAL LEONARD
BASS METHOD

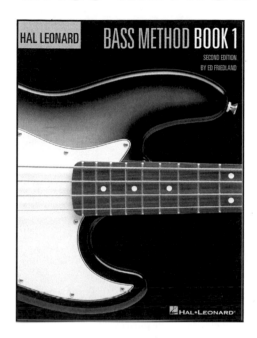

HAL LEONARD BASS METHOD BOOK 1
SECOND EDITION
BY ED FRIEDLAND

METHOD BOOKS

by Ed Friedland

BOOK 1 - 2ND EDITION
Book 1 teaches: tuning; playing position; musical symbols; notes within the first five frets; common bass lines, patterns and rhythms; rhythms through eighth notes; playing tips and techniques; more than 100 great songs, riffs and examples; and more! The audio includes 44 full-band tracks for demonstration or play-along.
00695067 Book Only................................... $9.99
00695068 Book/Online Audio............................... $14.99
01100122 Deluxe - Book/Online Audio/Video $19.99

BOOK 2 - 2ND EDITION
Book 2 continues where Book 1 left off and teaches: the box shape; moveable boxes; notes in fifth position; major and minor scales; the classic blues line; the shuffle rhythm; tablature; and more!
00695069 Book Only.................................... $9.99
00695070 Book/Online Audio............................... $14.99

BOOK 3 - 2ND EDITION
With the third book, progressing students will learn more great songs, riffs and examples; sixteenth notes; playing off chord symbols; slap and pop techniques; hammer-ons and pull-offs; playing different styles and grooves; and more.
00695071 Book Only.................................... $9.99
00695072 Book/Online Audio............................... $14.99

COMPOSITE - 2ND EDITION
This money-saving edition contains Books 1, 2 and 3.
00695073 Book Only... $19.99
00695074 Book/Online Audio............................... $27.99

DVD
Play your favorite songs in no time with this DVD! Covers: tuning, notes in first through third position, rhythms through eighth notes, fingerstyle and pick playing, 4/4 and 3/4 time, and more! Includes 6 full songs and on-screen music notation. 68 minutes.
00695849 DVD $19.95

BASS FOR KIDS
by Chad Johnson

Bass for Kids is a fun, easy course that teaches children to play bass guitar faster than ever before. Popular songs such as "Crazy Train," "Every Breath You Take," "A Hard Day's Night" and "Wild Thing" keep kids motivated, and the clean, simple page layouts ensure their attention remains focused on one concept at a time.
00696449 Book/Online Audio $14.99

REFERENCE BOOKS

BASS SCALE FINDER
by Chad Johnson

Learn to use the entire fretboard with the *Bass Scale Finder*. This book contains over 1,300 scale diagrams for the most important 17 scale types.
00695781 6" x 9" Edition.......................................$9.99
00695778 9" x 12" Edition...................................$10.99

BASS ARPEGGIO FINDER
by Chad Johnson

This extensive reference guide lays out over 1,300 arpeggio shapes. 28 different qualities are covered for each key, and each quality is presented in four different shapes.
00695817 6" x 9" Edition.......................................$9.99
00695816 9" x 12" Edition.....................................$9.99

MUSIC THEORY FOR BASSISTS
by Sean Malone

Acclaimed bassist and composer Sean Malone will explain the written language of music, using easy-to-understand terms and concepts, diagrams, and much more. The audio provides 96 tracks of examples, demonstrations, and play-alongs.
00695756 Book/Online Audio $19.99

STYLE BOOKS

BASS LICKS
by Ed Friedland

This comprehensive supplement to any bass method will help students learn over 200 great bass licks, lines and grooves in many rhythmic styles. *Bass Licks* illustrates how simple melodic patterns can become the springboard for group improvisation or the foundation of a song.
00696035 Book/Online Audio $15.99

BASS LINES
by Matt Scharfglass

500 expertly written bass lines, riffs and fills in a wide variety of musical genres are included in this comprehensive collection to help players expand their bass vocabulary. The examples cover many tempos, keys and feels, and include easy bass lines for beginners on up to advanced riffs for more experienced bassists.
00148194 Book/Online Audio $22.99

BLUES BASS
by Ed Friedland

Learn to play studying the songs of B.B. King, Stevie Ray Vaughan, Muddy Waters, Albert King, the Allman Brothers, T-Bone Walker, and many more. Learn riffs from blues classics including: Born Under a Bad Sign • Hideaway • Hoochie Coochie Man • Killing Floor • Pride and Joy • Sweet Home Chicago • The Thrill Is Gone • and more.
00695870 Book/Online Audio $17.99

COUNTRY BASS
by Glenn Letsch

21 songs, including: Act Naturally • Boot Scootin' Boogie • Crazy • Honky Tonk Man • Love You Out Loud • Luckenbach, Texas (Back to the Basics of Love) • No One Else on Earth • Ring of Fire • Southern Nights • Streets of Bakersfield • Whose Bed Have Your Boots Been Under? • and more.
00695928 Book/Online Audio $22.99

FRETLESS BASS
by Chris Kringel

18 songs, including: Bad Love • Continuum • Even Flow • Everytime You Go Away • Hocus Pocus • I Could Die for You • Jelly Roll • King of Pain • Kiss of Life • Lady in Red • Tears in Heaven • Very Early • What I Am • White Room • more.
00695850..$22.99

FUNK BASS
by Chris Kringel

This is your complete guide to learning the basics of grooving and soloing funk bass. Songs include: Can't Stop • I'll Take You There • Let's Groove • Stay • What Is Hip • and more.
00695792 Book/Online Audio...............................$22.99

R&B BASS
by Glenn Letsch

This book/audio pack uses actual classic R&B, Motown, soul and funk songs to teach you how to groove in the style of James Jamerson, Bootsy Collins, Bob Babbitt, and many others. The 19 songs include: For Once in My Life • Knock on Wood • Mustang Sally • Respect • Soul Man • Stand by Me • and more.
00695823 Book/Online Audio $19.99

ROCK BASS
by Sean Malone

This book/audio pack uses songs from a myriad of rock genres to teach the key elements of rock bass. Includes: Another One Bites the Dust • Beast of Burden • Money • Roxanne • Smells like Teen Spirit • and more.
00695801 Book/Online Audio...............................$22.99

SUPPLEMENTARY SONGBOOKS

These great songbooks correlate with Books 1-3 of the *Hal Leonard Bass Method*, giving students great songs to play while they're still learning! The audio tracks include great accompaniment and demo tracks.

EASY POP BASS LINES
20 great songs that students in Book 1 can master. Includes: Come as You Are • Crossfire • Great Balls of Fire • Imagine • Surfin' U.S.A. • Takin' Care of Business • Wild Thing • and more.
00695809 Book/Online Audio................................$16.99

MORE EASY POP BASS LINES
20 great songs for Level 2 students. Includes: Bad, Bad Leroy Brown • Crazy Train • I Heard It Through the Grapevine • My Generation • Pride and Joy • Ramblin' Man • Summer of '69 • and more.
00695819 Book Only.......................................$14.99
00695818 Book/Online Audio...............................$16.99

EVEN MORE EASY POP BASS LINES
20 great songs for Level 3 students, including: ABC • Another One Bites the Dust • Brick House • Come Together • Higher Ground • Iron Man • The Joker • Sweet Emotion • Under Pressure • more.
00695821 Book $14.99
00695820 Book/Online Audio...............................$16.99

HAL•LEONARD

Visit Hal Leonard online at
www.halleonard.com

Prices, contents and availability subject to change without notice.
Some products may not be available outside of U.S.A.

BASS RECORDED VERSIONS

   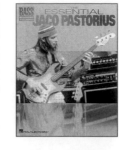 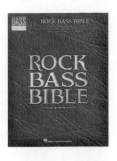

Bass Recorded Versions feature authentic transcriptions written in standard notation and tablature for bass guitar. This series features complete bass lines from the classics to contemporary superstars.

25 Essential Rock Bass Classics
00690210 / $19.99

Avenged Sevenfold – Nightmare
00691054 / $19.99

The Beatles – Abbey Road
00128336 / $24.99

The Beatles – 1962-1966
00690556 / $19.99

The Beatles – 1967-1970
00690557 / $24.99

Best of Bass Tab
00141806 / $17.99

The Best of Blink 182
00690549 / $18.99

Blues Bass Classics
00690291 / $22.99

Boston – Bass Collection
00690935 / $19.95

Stanley Clarke – Collection
00672307 / $22.99

Dream Theater – Bass Anthology
00119345 / $29.99

Funk Bass Bible
00690744 / $27.99

Hard Rock Bass Bible
00690746 / $22.99

Jimi Hendrix – Are You Experienced?
00690371 / $17.95

Jimi Hendrix – Bass Tab Collection
00160505 / $24.99

Iron Maiden – Bass Anthology
00690867 / $24.99

Jazz Bass Classics
00102070 / $19.99

The Best of Kiss
00690080 / $22.99

Lynyrd Skynyrd – All-Time Greatest Hits
00690956 / $24.99

Bob Marley – Bass Collection
00690568 / $24.99

Mastodon – Crack the Skye
00691007 / $19.99

Megadeth – Bass Anthology
00691191 / $22.99

Metal Bass Tabs
00103358 / $22.99

Best of Marcus Miller
00690811 / $29.99

Motown Bass Classics
00690253 / $19.99

Muse – Bass Tab Collection
00123275 / $22.99

Nirvana – Bass Collection
00690066 / $19.99

Nothing More – Guitar & Bass Collection
00265439 / $24.99

The Offspring – Greatest Hits
00690809 / $17.95

The Essential Jaco Pastorius
00690420 / $22.99

Jaco Pastorius – Greatest Jazz Fusion Bass Player
00690421 / $24.99

Pearl Jam – Ten
00694882 / $22.99

Pink Floyd – Dark Side of the Moon
00660172 / $19.99

The Best of Police
00660207 / $24.99

Pop/Rock Bass Bible
00690747 / $24.99

Queen – The Bass Collection
00690065 / $22.99

R&B Bass Bible
00690745 / $24.99

Rage Against the Machine
00690248 / $22.99

Red Hot Chili Peppers – BloodSugarSexMagik
00690064 / $22.99

Red Hot Chili Peppers – By the Way
00690585 / $24.99

Red Hot Chili Peppers – Californication
00690390 / $22.99

Red Hot Chili Peppers – Greatest Hits
00690675 / $22.99

Red Hot Chili Peppers – I'm with You
00691167 / $22.99

Red Hot Chili Peppers – One Hot Minute
00690091 / $22.99

Red Hot Chili Peppers – Stadium Arcadium
00690853 / Book Only $24.95

Rock Bass Bible
00690446 / $22.99

Rolling Stones – Bass Collection
00690256 / $24.99

Royal Blood
00151826 / $24.99

Rush – The Spirit of Radio: Greatest Hits 1974-1987
00323856 / $24.99

Best of Billy Sheehan
00173972 / $24.99

Slap Bass Bible
00159716 / $29.99

Sly & The Family Stone for Bass
00109733 / $24.99

Best of Yes
00103044 / $24.99

Best of ZZ Top for Bass
00691069 / $24.99

Visit Hal Leonard Online at
www.halleonard.com